P9-AFR-617

Herbert, Mike
Michael Jordan

DO NOT REMOVE
CARDS FROM POCKET

OCT 2 8 1993

DEMCO

Sports Stars

MICHAEL JORDAN

The Bull's Air Power

By Mike Herbert

CHILDRENS PRESS®
CHICAGO

Cover photograph: Focus On Sports
Inside photographs courtesy of the following:
Brian G. Fritz, pages 6 and 18
Carl V. Sissac, pages 9, 22, 24, 27, 28, 38, and 40
Ira Golden, pages 10, 12, 20, 30, and 34
Bryan Yablonsky, page 14
Vic Milton, page 17
Betsy Peabody Rowe, pages 25 and 33
Northwest Indiana Chevy Dealers, page 36
Wilson Sporting Goods, page 42

Library of Congress Cataloging in Publication Data

Herbert, Mike.
    Michael Jordan: the Bull's air power.

    (Sport stars)
    Summary: Examines the career of the Chicago Bulls
basketball player who has been described as unstoppable on
the court.
    1. Jordan, Michael, 1963-   —Juvenile literature.
2. Basketball players—United States—Biography—Juvenile
literature. [1. Jordan, Michael, 1963-
2. Basketball players. 3. Afro-Americans—Biography]
I. Title. II. Series.
GV884.J67H47 1987   796.32'3'0924 [B] [92] 87-20868
ISBN 0-516-04362-5

    4 5 6 7 8 9 10 R 96 95 94 93

Sports Stars

MICHAEL JORDAN

The Bull's Air Power

Michael Jordan. Air Jordan. Air Power!

Michael Jordan is the most exciting basketball player in the world.

Everyone loves Michael Jordan. He smiles. He laughs. He is so happy when he plays basketball. He makes everyone who watches him happy, too.

Michael plays for the Chicago Bulls. He is a pro in the National Basketball Association. He gets paid to play basketball. But he would play for free. That's because he loves the game so much.

Michael plays more exciting basketball than anyone else. He can jump higher than anyone. He can slam the dunk shot and make the fans scream. Everyone has fun when Michael Jordan plays.

Michael is the best. Everyone feels it when Michael dunks. But, he can do more than dunks. He can dip. He can soar. He can double-pump.

Michael is a clean-cut, happy-go-lucky new hero for America.

Michael Jeffery Jordan was born February 17, 1963 in Brooklyn, New York. He grew up in Wilmington, North Carolina. He has two sisters, Deloris and Rosylyn, and two brothers, Larry and James. Michael went to Laney High School in Wilmington.

Basketball is exciting when Michael plays.

Sitting on the training table

"I played baseball, football, and track, trying to find the right place for my talents," Michael says. "As I grew, I found the best target was the basketball court."

But in the beginning, Michael was not a good player. As a sophomore he was cut from the varsity team.

"I was angry, hurt, embarrassed, and ticked off," Michael says. "I spent that whole next summer in the gym, working to get better. I had something to prove to myself. It probably was good that it happened to me."

Michael grew from 5 feet 11 to 6 feet 3. But he was not a star yet.

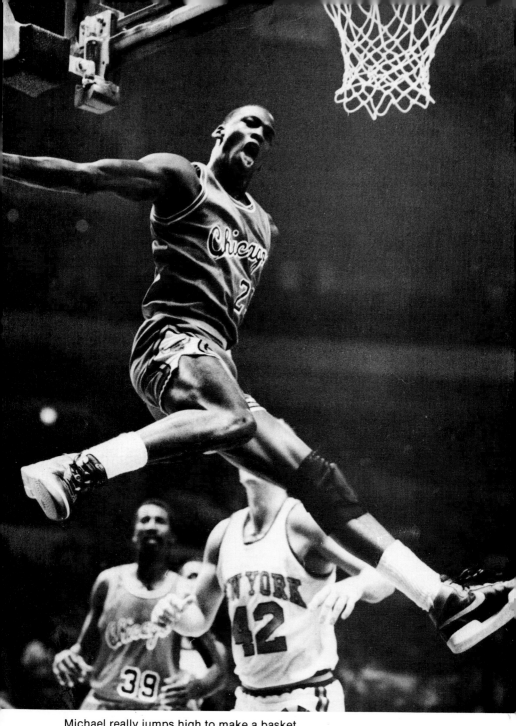

Michael really jumps high to make a basket.

Michael tells his story: "Next year I make the team, barely. I'm like the 15th man. My goal is to play at a Division I college, but no one from Wilmington ever went to one. I'm living on hope. But then I get accepted at the Five Star Basketball Camp in Pittsburgh, the best camp in the nation for high schoolers. That's when I feel like someone has tapped me on the shoulder and said, 'You must emerge as somebody—somebody to be admired, to achieve big things. But don't lose your identity.'

"Then I'm steered to [the University of] North Carolina and it suits me perfectly. The coaches don't baby you. They make you work, set goals, achieve. And my parents are very smart. They kept me involved in my education, made sure I

Dean Smith, the coach from North Carolina, is the second from the right.

was disciplined, that I knew right from wrong, that I didn't get involved with alcohol or drugs."

At North Carolina, Michael became a real star. As a freshman, he made the first basket in his first game of the year. But everyone remembers his last basket of the year. When Michael made it, there were 15 seconds left to go in the game. It won the NCAA Championship for his team. Now he was really a star!

"I learned from Coach [Dean] Smith that basketball is really a team game," Michael says. "In high school, it seems like you're more concerned with personal numbers. In college, I learned that personal stuff is empty if it doesn't help the team win. And if you think you're too important, the team suffers."

In 1984, Michael was chosen to be the captain of the United States Olympic basketball team. They won a gold medal. Also, he was named the college player of the year. He was an All-American.

Michael gives credit to his coach, Dean Smith. "He is devoted to developing his players, not only as athletes, but as men in all walks of life. He matured me way beyond basketball and I owe him an awful lot for that."

After his junior year of college, Michael decided to become a pro. He was the third college player chosen by the pro teams. He became a Chicago Bull. He was then 6 feet 6.

In 1984, Michael was picked by the Chicago Bulls.

After his first season, Michael was chosen as rookie of the year.

Michael's first year was a huge success. Only two players scored more points than he did. Michael was the only player in the league to score in double figures in all 82 games. He was the highest-scoring rookie since Kareem Abdul-Jabbar. And Michael was fourth in the league in steals. But more important, Michael was a hit with the fans. Everyone loved the way he played.

At the end of the year, Michael was voted the rookie of the year. He joined the ranks of recent great players. He was in with players such as Ralph Sampson, Terry Cummings, and Larry Bird. Michael had made 2,313 points. He had averaged 28.2 points per game. He also had 534 rebounds and 481 assists. He made more than 51 percent of his shots.

Michael shoots a jumper.

Michael started his second season as a Chicago Bull with more success. It looked as if it was going to be a great year. But in the third game, Michael broke his left foot.

For the first time in his life, Michael missed a basketball game. He had to sit out almost all of the season. Then near the end of the season, Michael complained. He wanted to play. He said the Bulls' owners wouldn't let him play. He insisted he play. He could hurt his foot again, but he wanted to play.

With Michael's help, the Bulls just barely made the playoffs. They had to face the Boston Celtics. But that didn't scare Michael. He played the game of his life. He scored 49 points! The Celtics won, but they couldn't stop Michael.

Michael on the way to slam dunking.

The next game, the Celtics had to stop Michael. But they couldn't do it. Michael scored 63 points! It was the most points ever scored in a playoff game. But the Celtics went on to win the championship.

Superstar Larry Bird said later, "He's God disguised as Michael Jordan."

On the first day of the 1986-87 season, Michael scored 50 points. Later, he scored 50 points in three straight games. Once, he scored 61!

"I've never thought of myself as unstoppable, but I felt really close to it," Michael said of that night against the Detroit Pistons. "I was as close as possible. During that stretch I was coming up with shots that a lot of people hadn't seen, shots that I hadn't seen. They were just going down."

Defending against Kevin McHale of the Celtics

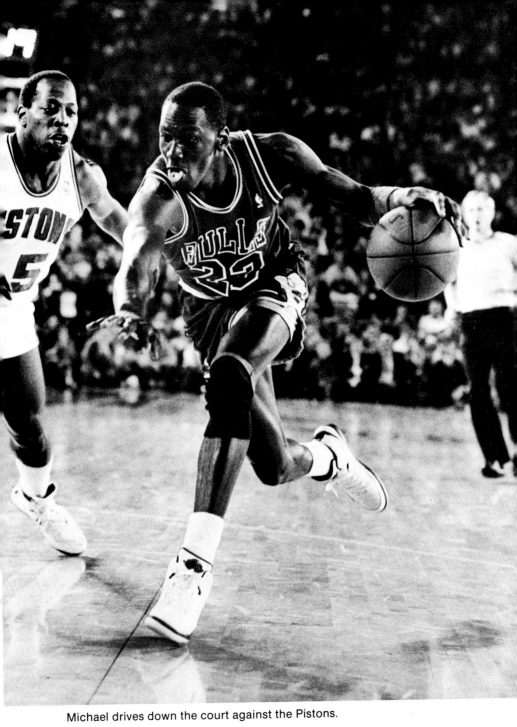

Michael drives down the court against the Pistons.

In one game against the Atlanta Hawks, Michael scored a record 23 consecutive points!

At the NBA All-Star Game, Michael entered the Slam Dunk contest. Of course, he won that, too!

At the end of the amazing season, he was named to the All-NBA team. Akeem Olajuwon of the Houston Rockets was at center. The forwards were Larry Bird and Kevin McHale of the Boston Celtics. The other guard was Magic Johnson of the world champion Los Angeles Lakers.

Some people said the Bulls played Michael too much, and he worked so hard, he was burned out.

The 1987 Slam Dunk Champion

Michael takes a well-earned rest.

"I never thought I was burned out," said Michael. "I don't worry about burning out. . . . I can only play one speed—that's all out. You can't give any less in this league. There's too much talent."

How do you try to stop Michael Jordan? One pro team scout simply said, "You cannot stop him when he goes to the basket." Yes, in the air Michael is Air Jordan. He is the Bull's Air Power.

The fans come to see Michael play. The Bulls broke all their attendance records. Before Michael joined the team, the Bulls averaged 6,365 fans a game. With Michael, the average is 11,887.

A reverse slam dunk

Everyone likes Michael—his fans, his teammates, and his opponents.

Superstar Julius Erving said, "At 23, he had much more poise than I had at that age. The sky's the limit for Michael."

Says former coach Doug Collins: "He can post up down low. He can shoot the jumper. You can lob it to him. You can isolate with him. You can put him in the stack. You can put him anywhere in the offense and he'll find a way to score."

Says Dominque Wilkins of the Atlanta Hawks, "There's no way to stop him. No matter what you do, he is going to find a way to get the shot off."

Says Bill Brown, producer of the television show "60 Minutes," which featured Michael, "He's a phenomenon—handsome, educated, dedicated, a very decent person. Despite the extraordinary athletic prowess, sudden fame, and financial success, this kid is still unaffected by it all."

And how does Michael respond to all this praise?

"What drives me are challenges," he says. "I remember when I was in high school. I thought, 'Gee, if I can just make it to a small college.' Well, people had huge expectations of me when I came into the NBA.

Michael scores over Laimbeer, with the Detroit Pistons.

Relaxing before the game

"I'm here because I love the game, I want to have fun, and because it's important to me to use all of my ability.

"I've seen what success can do to people. There is no way I'll change. I know who I am, where I've been, and the gifts I've been given. My influences have been too solid to have me losing my head over some success. Some take it for granted. But I know that I'm a fortunate person. I won't let myself blow this.

"It's great that fans admire my style so much. I'm not going to do anything to disappoint them."

What is the personal side of Michael Jordan like?

Michael endorses a number of products, including Chevrolet.

Michael is sensitive, thoughtful, and unfazed by success. He is charming, modest, open, and sincere. He always wears a smile. He is polite. He has fun. He is an elegant dresser. Michael loves kids. He encourages youngsters to read. He says he reads, "about 23 books a year."

One Halloween, Michael was upset because the Bulls were playing in New York. So, he left a note taped on the door of his house. The note said, "Dear Kids: I'll be back in three days if you want to trick-or-treat. Michael Jordan."

Michael cares about people, too. He supports charities and programs to help people. One of the campaigns he cares most about is "Say No To Drugs." Some athletes think drugs can help

Kids are important to Michael. He also works on the "Say No To Drugs" campaign.

them. But Michael tells everyone he meets to stay away from drugs because drugs kill people.

Once, when he was visiting a children's hospital, Michael wrote a check for $15,000 on the spur of the moment.

When Michael isn't playing basketball, he likes to play golf. He is very good. He is so good he can play with the pros. "Putting is a lot like shooting free throws," he says. "It's all concentration and technique."

Michael combines his love for people and sports by sponsoring charity golf tournaments. These tournaments have raised money for causes such as the United Negro College Fund and the Ronald McDonald House for seriously ill children. He says, "I'm always willing to give

"This is probably the easiest job in America," says Michael.

my time to help set positive guidelines and set a positive road for kids to follow to achieve dreams and do well in society."

He also runs the Michael Jordan Basketball Camp. He recently was an actor in a film called, *Heaven is a Playground*, about basketball.

"I'm not an actor," he says, "and I may be the biggest flop, but someday I can tell my kid, 'I did a movie.'"

He also is studying to get his college degree.

"My main priority is to help the Bulls win basketball games," Michael says. "But within that context I try to use my God-given talent to entertain and give the fans something extra. When they leave the arena, I'd like for them to feel like they saw something special.

"I'm so fortunate to get paid for doing what I love. This is probably the easiest job in America.

"I firmly believe that if your desire is strong, you can do anything."

In 1987-88 Michael continued to dominate the NBA. He won the league MVP Award. He won

the Defensive Player of the Year Award. He won the All-NBA First Team Guard Award. He was the All-Star Game MVP. He was the All-Star Slam Dunk champion. For the second year in a row he was the highest-scoring player in the league, with 35 points a game. He was unbelievable!

And the next season Michael was just as good. He continued to break records for his team and for the entire league. He signed a deal to make $19 million over the next seven years with endorsements. That didn't include any of his pay for playing basketball—just doing commercials.

Advertising also gave Michael something else—a new wife! Michael met Juanita Vanoy at a Chicago ad agency where she worked when he came to discuss endorsements. After dating for several years, they were married in September 1989 in a Las Vegas wedding chapel. Michael and Juanita have two young sons—Jeffrey and Marcus—and a daughter, Jasmine.

Raising a family the right way takes a lot of time. It is very important to Michael to raise a family in the way he was raised. But Michael still wants to help other people and worthy causes, too. To accomplish these two goals, he established the Michael Jordan Foundation. The foundation employs people who can organize and consolidate Michael's work for charity, so that he can spend more time with his family.

And, the most amazing thing is that he still keeps smiling. Michael is just a good guy. He says his hero is his brother, Larry. "He used to beat me one-on-one a lot when I was a kid, and it inspired me to perfect my game," he says.

In the 1990-91 season, Michael won the MVP award for the second time. He led the NBA for the fifth straight year, with a 31.5 points-per-game average, and also led the Bulls in all-time points with 16,596. And, too, the Bulls became the champions of the NBA, making this a particularly spectacular year.

In 1991-92, Michael won the MVP award for

the third time. And once again, he was the NBA statistical leader, averaging 30.1 points, 6.4 rebounds, and 6.1 assists per game. But Michael's greatest accomplishment of the season was leading the Bulls to their second straight NBA championship. Then, on the heels of this victory, Michael traveled to Barcelona, Spain, to play on the "Dream Team"—the gold-medal-winning 1992 U.S. Olympic men's basketball team.

Michael Jordan has taken life to the limit. To new heights. Air Jordan is as high as it can ever get.

CHRONOLOGY

1963—Michael Jeffery Jordan is born on February 17 in Brooklyn, New York, the son of Deloris and James Jordan.

1981—Michael graduates from Laney High School in Wilmington, North Carolina, where he was a standout basketball player his junior and senior years.

—Michael receives a basketball scholarship to play at the University of North Carolina under respected coach Dean Smith.

1982—Michael scores the basket that beats Georgetown University to win the NCAA Championship.

1983—Michael is selected to the first team All-American Team at the end of the season. He is also named the College Player of the Year.

1984—Michael is again named the College Player of the Year. He leads the Atlantic Coast Conference in scoring.

—Michael is the leading scorer on the United States Pan American team, which won a gold medal.

—Michael is co-captain of the Men's United States Olympic basketball team, coached by Bob Knight. He averages 17.1 points a game, and the team wins a gold medal.

—Michael decides to leave college, and he is drafted by the Chicago Bulls as the third player taken in the 1984 draft, behind Akeem Olajuwan and Sam Bowie.

1985—Michael is voted a starting guard on the Eastern Conference All-Star Team.

—Scoring more points (2,213) than any other player in the NBA, Michael is voted the NBA Rookie of the Year. He is the only player in the league to score in double figures in all 82 games. He also has 534 rebounds, 481 assists, and makes more than 51 percent of his shots.

—In the third game of the 1985-86 season, Michael breaks the navicular tarsal bone in his left foot and misses 64 games. But he comes back at the end of the season, helps his Bulls reach the playoffs, and scores a record 135 points in three playoff games against the Boston Celtics. His 63 points in double overtime set an NBA playoff record. Nevertheless, the Bulls lose 135 to 131, and the Celtics go on to win the NBA Championship.

1987—Michael is the first player in league history to have more than 100 blocked shots and more than 200 steals. He scores more than 3,000 points. He plays in his second All-Star Game. He wins the Slam Dunk contest. Michael is named to the NBA All-Star Team. The Bulls reach the playoffs, but lose again to the Celtics.

1988—Michael wins every major NBA award—league MVP, Defensive Player of the Year, All-NBA First Team, All-Defensive First Team, All-Star Game MVP, All-Star Slam Dunk Champion. He wins the league scoring title. He leads the league in steals. He led the Bulls into the playoffs, and set records defeating Cleveland and in losing to Detroit. He led the team in scoring in every game.

1989—Michael leads the Bulls again. He again is named the league Most Valuable Player. He again leads the league in scoring. The Bulls lose again in the playoffs because they are not that good a team, but Michael continues to be the team star.

—On September 2, Michael marries Juanita Vanoy in Las Vegas.

1990—Michael leads the Chicago Bulls into the playoffs for the fifth straight year. He is the league leader in points scored (2,753, or 33.6 points per game) for the fourth straight year. He also leads the league in steals.

—On March 28, Michael scores 69 points against the Cleveland Cavaliers, the ninth highest point total for a regular season game in NBA history.

—Michael becomes the all-time leading scorer of the Chicago Bulls with 14,016 career points.

1991—Michael wins the MVP award for the second time.

—Michael leads the league with a 31.5 points-per-game average.

—Michael leads the Bulls with 16,596 points—an all-time record.

—Bulls become NBA champions.

—A second son, Marcus, is born in January 1991.

1992—Michael wins the MVP award for the third time and for the second year in a row. He is the NBA statistical leader, averaging 30.1 points, 6.4 rebounds, and 6.1 assists per game. He is a starter in the NBA All Star Game, and leads the Bulls to their second straight NBA championship.

—Michael wins a gold medal as a member of the "Dream Team"—the men's U.S. Olympic basketball team at the 1992 Summer Olympics in Barcelona, Spain.

—A daughter, Jasmine, is born in December.

ABOUT THE AUTHOR

Mike Herbert is a sports magazine editor. He has written and edited sports for 20 years. The magazines he edits are written for sports fans. The are: *Inside Sports, Basketball Digest, Bowling Digest, Football Digest, Hockey Digest, Soccer Digest, Auto Racing Digest,* and *Baseball Digest.* He is lucky enough to be able to see many of Michael Jordan's basketball games.

Before he was a magazine editor, Mr. Herbert was a newspaper sports reporter for the *Chicago Tribune,* and a high school English teacher and coach. He also played sports in high school and college. He has always loved sports. He still plays sports, especially golf.

Mr Herbert is the author of another title in the Sports Stars series: *Mike Schmidt: The Human Vacuum Cleaner.*

Mr. Herbert lives in Naperville, Illinois, with his family. His wife, Lana, and Mr. Herbert both enjoy golf. They have two daughters. Nancy is a college student who wants to be a teacher. Susie is a high school soccer player.